Yosemite
on my mind

JEFF FOOTT

" *When asked why Yosemite is so important to me, I always begin with a simple declaration: It is The Place…. Yosemite scenery stuns, even overwhelms the senses. Nowhere else is nature so monumentally present.* "

David Robertson

FALCON®

From Glacier Point, the commanding view takes in Yosemite Valley,
Half Dome, and the High Sierras. LONDIE G. PADELSKY

" *It is as if Nature had here put herself to show a parable of contrasted excellences, setting the stern heights and solemn silences of the cliffs against the soft demeanor and gentle voices of trees and flowers, streams and heavenly meadows; and to marry them together she pours the great waterfalls, in whose cloudy graces majesty and loveliness are so mingled that one cannot tell which of the two delights him the more.* "

J. Smeaton Chase

A golden eagle surveys its domain. LEE KLINE

Cathedral Rock looms above the Merced River, offering spiritual rejuvenation to those who seek its sanctuary. LONDIE G. PADELSKY

Just out of the chute, the Merced River thunders almost 600 feet down precipitous Nevada Fall. LONDIE G. PADELSKY

Heralds of the High Sierra's brief summer season, wildflowers carpet a meadow on Mount Dana. KATHLEEN NORRIS COOK

" The alpine tundra is a land of contrast and incredible intensity, where the sky is the size of forever and the flowers the size of a millisecond. "

Ann H. Zwinger

Penstemons are common at all elevations in Yosemite. LONDIE G. PADELSKY

A western juniper interrupts the colorful interplay of light and water on the Tuolumne River. JEFF FOOTT

The whole wilderness seems to be alive and familiar, full of humanity. The very stones seem talkative, sympathetic, brotherly.

John Muir

Like its relative the raccoon, the ringtail is primarily nocturnal. CLAUDE STEELMAN

Glaciers carried these boulders, called *erratics*, from their original sites and scattered them as carelessly as a child does toys. JEFF GNASS

Backpackers orient themselves at Merced Lake. LONDIE G. PADELSKY

JOHN MUIR TRAIL

DONOHUE PASS 11.3
MERCED LAKE 14.1
YOSEMITE VALLEY 26.9

TUOLUMNE PASS 5.5
VOGELSANG 6.1

The popular John Muir Trail extends 211 miles through
the heart of the Sierra. LONDIE G. PADELSKY

A horse packer negotiates cobblestone switchbacks en route to the Vogelsang High Sierra Camp. LONDIE G. PADELSKY

The setting sun saves its last caress for the timeworn face of Half Dome. THOMAS E. GAMACHE

" The Half-Dome possesses one feature in particular that I always found remarkable and charming,— the strange manner in which it catches and holds the last light of the day... and like a great heliograph reflects the peaceful messages of the evening over all the quiet valley. "

J. Smeaton Chase

A cable route allows hikers to climb hand over hand up the steep northeast slope of Half Dome. JOHN DITTLI

" *Whoever climbs to the summits of the Sierra will know why prophets have always sought mountaintops to commune with their gods. A strong, clear light falls on a frozen tableau: massive rock on massive rock with scattered lakelets to interrupt the vast cold emptiness.* "

Ezra Bowen

From the Half Dome cable route, climbers can see monolithic Clouds Rest
looming above the valley floor. KENNAN WARD

A cyclist mixes sightseeing with exercise as she pedals along a paved bikeway. LAURENCE PARENT

" The air up there... is very pure and fine, bracing and delicious. And why shouldn't it be?—it is the same the angels breath."

Mark Twain

Stately trees line the path to Yosemite Falls.
RICHARD HAMILTON SMITH

Cow parsnips frame 1,430-foot Upper Yosemite Fall. JEFF GNASS

Wildcat Creek bounds gracefully down a series of uneven stone steps. KATHLEEN NORRIS COOK

Bridalveil Creek, shrouded in mist, tumbles through a battlement of boulders.   LAURENCE PARENT

" No feature... of all the noble landscape as seen from here seems more wonderful than the Cathedral itself, a temple displaying Nature's best masonry and sermons in stones. "

John Muir

A yellow-bellied marmot is ready to sound the alert. KENNAN WARD

The rugged face of Cathedral Peak contrasts with the glacially polished granite that rims Cathedral Lake. LONDIE G. PADELSKY

The tiny blossoms of miner's lettuce reach skyward around the discarded cone of a sugar pine.   KATHLEEN NORRIS COOK

" Wandering into the heart of the mountains, we find a new world, and stand beside the majestic pines and firs and sequoias silent and awestricken, as if in the presence of superior beings new arrived from some other star, so calm and bright and godlike they are."

John Muir

Separated in age by centuries, a young "witchy-haired" sequoia grows up in the shadow of an older relative.   LARRY ULRICH

Fern Spring bubbles up through the forest floor, then gently descends toward the Merced River. JEFF FOOTT

Close to 300 black bears roam the confines of Yosemite National Park, exciting visitors who catch one of their rare appearances. KENNAN WARD

" Bears are *wilderness—the element that must be there in order to have a complete natural scheme. It would not be wild without them.* "

Gary Brown

A lone coyote scouts the edge of a managed burn for an opportunistic meal. RON SANFORD

" Each season brings a world of enjoyment and interest in the watching of its unfolding, its gradual, harmonious development, its culminating graces—and just as one begins to tire of it, it passes away and a radical change comes, with new witcheries and new glories in its train. And I think that to one in sympathy with nature, each season, in its turn, seems the loveliest. "

Mark Twain

Fiery oak leaves and bracken fern fronds signal the advance of autumn.
LONDIE G. PADELSKY

A bigleaf maple makes a colorful contribution to the collage of detritus on the forest floor.   LONDIE G. PADELSKY

Sentinel Rock watches over a placid stretch of the Merced River.   LARRY ULRICH

The great horned owl breeds and nests in Yosemite.
SHERM SPOELSTRA

" *In the autumn the sighing of the winds is softer than ever, the gentle ah-ah-ing filling the sky with a fine universal mist of music, the birds have little to say, and there is no appreciable stir or rustling among the trees save that caused by the harvesting squirrels.* "

John Muir

A dusting of fresh snow brightens the timeless grandeur of Yosemite Valley. WILLIAM NEILL / LARRY ULRICH STOCK

> **"** *I find the winter wilderness not a cabinet full of dried specimens, but a rich and peaceable kingdom of creatures and growing things, each meeting the daily hardships of cold weather in his own way, or simply sleeping until, with spring, the living is easier.* **"**

Ezra Bowen

A scrub jay fluffs its feathers to ward off the morning chill.   KEN ARCHER

The Merced River wears an image of Half Dome in a locket of calm water. JEFF GNASS

Clouds encircle the brow of El Capitan, 3,000 feet above the valley floor.   WILLIAM NEILL / LARRY ULRICH STOCK

Ice forms interrupt the dance between sunset and water.   JOHN DITTLI

Meadows and mountains slumber under a quilt of snow at Tioga Pass. LARRY CARVER

" *The familiar and intimate aspects of the Sierra that one has learned to love during the long summer days are not obscured by winter snows. Rather the grand contours and profiles of the range are clarified and embellished under the white splendor; the mountains are possessed of a new majesty and peace.* "

Ansel Adams

Backcountry skiers find enchantment in Yosemite's winter wonderland. JOHN DITTLI

An ice climber picks his way up a frozen waterfall in
Lee Vining Canyon. JOHN DITTLI

And how glorious the shining after the short summer showers and after frosty nights when the morning sunbeams are pouring through the crystals on the grass and pine needles, and how ineffably spiritually fine is the morning-glow on the mountain-tops and the alpenglow of evening. Well may the Sierra be named, not the Snowy Range, but the Range of Light.

John Muir

Painted by the setting sun, a watery canvas silhouettes a packer as he leads his string home. LONDIE G. PADELSKY

Reminders of another era linger in the shadow of Mount Lewis. DENNIS FLAHERTY

Vogelsang High Sierra Camp is such a popular destination that reservations are required.
LONDIE G. PADELSKY

A cabin window at the abandoned Great Sierra mine frames a picture of Gaylor Lakes. JOHN DITTLI

A pika gathers summer greenery, dries it, and piles it into haystacks for winter consumption.
SHERM SPOELSTRA

The Yosemite Chapel offers a house of worship within the hallowed walls of Yosemite Valley. JEFF FOOTT

The grandeur of the Ahwahnee Hotel complements the magnificence of Yosemite Valley. LAURENCE PARENT

Opened in 1927, the Ahwahnee Hotel offers grand accommodations. THOMAS E. GAMACHE

A sightseer contemplates the raw power and sheer elegance of Nevada Fall. CHRISTIAN HEEB / GNASS PHOTO IMAGES

Smiles come easy after a refreshing summer dip in the Merced River. LONDIE G. PADELSKY

Floaters find peace on the Merced River within earshot of tumultuous Upper Yosemite Fall. THOMAS E. GAMACHE

Holding forth in the world's greatest classroom, a park ranger leads a discussion on the power of erosion.
CHRISTIAN HEEB / GNASS PHOTO IMAGES

6 6 *It just didn't seem like a complete year unless I went to Yosemite.* 9 9

Jack Phinney

Meadow reclamation involves the occasional signing and frequent pulling of weeds. LONDIE G. PADELSKY

A park naturalist shares her wealth of knowledge about Yosemite's wonders with a group of visitors. LONDIE G. PADELSKY

The late legendary naturalist Carl Sharsmith invites visitors to explore the intricacies of a meadow carpet. KENNAN WARD

A boulder rests in a glacial tarn, deposited there by the very glacier that carved its final resting spot. JOHN DITTLI

At Olmsted Point, glacial polish and scattered erratics are stark reminders of Yosemite's geologic past. CHRISTIAN HEEB / GNASS PHOTO IMAGES

The fractured granite of Olmsted Point provides a shallow seed bed for this Jeffrey pine.

A sunset over Tuolomne Meadows proves that not all California gold is found underground. KATHLEEN NORRIS COOK

" *And the dawns and sunrises and sundowns of these mountain days,—the rose light creeping higher among the stars, changing to daffodil yellow, the level beams bursting forth, streaming across the ridges, touching pine after pine, awakening and warming all the mighty host to do gladly their shining day's work. The great sun-gold noons, the alabaster cloud-mountains, the landscape beaming with consciousness like the face of a god. The sunsets, when the trees stood hushed awaiting their good-night blessings. Divine, enduring, unwastable wealth.* "

John Muir

A mule deer enjoys the tranquility of first light. KEN ARCHER

Vegetable outshines mineral in this Yosemite Valley meadow. LAURENCE PARENT

Adorned by lichens, a white alder and granite boulder become one. WILLIAM NEILL / LARRY ULRICH STOCK

Mount Conness stands in silent testimony to the endurance of granite over glacier. JOHN DITTLI

Sunset bathes the escarpments below the summit of Mount Hoffman. WILLIAM NEILL / LARRY ULRICH STOCK

Climb the mountains and get their good tidings. Nature's peace will flow into you as sunshine flows into trees. The winds will blow their own freshness into you, and the storms their energy, while cares will drop off like autumn leaves.

John Muir

A Pacific tree frog races its shadow across the sun-kissed waters of Soda Springs. KENNAN WARD

A cowboy and his pack string ford the Lyell Fork of the Tuolumne River. LONDIE G. PADELSKY

> *What glorious landscapes are about me, new plants, new animals, new crystals, and multitudes of new mountains...—a glory day of admission into a new realm of wonders as if Nature had wooingly whispered, 'Come higher.'*

John Muir

After centuries of grinding acorns here, early inhabitants wore mortarlike pockets into this granite boulder. LONDIE G. PADELSKY

6 6 We... know above all else that our ability to regenerate ourselves emotionally and spiritually depends on the existence of places such as Yosemite, where we can witness the glory of nature and partake of its power. 9 9

David Robertson

A flint knapper works a piece of obsidian to a fine point. KENNAN WARD

A bark-thatched dwelling called an *u-mu-cha* shelters the legacy of Yosemite's Ahwahneechee Indians. DENNIS FLAHERTY

Bracken ferns on the shores of Siesta Lake dress for their autumnal slumber. LARRY ULRICH

" Broadleaf maples and oaks paint the landscape with russet, copper and gold. The dogwoods flash their salmon-pink when the sun touches their delicate leaves, and the pines, firs and incense-cedars hold their steady green in the symphony of color. "

Lewis P. Mansfield

The road to winter first winds through fall.
KATHLEEN NORRIS COOK

Indian hemp, named for its use as cordage, binds together autumn colors and the still waters of the Merced River. JEFF GNASS

A tree relinquishes its snowy crown as morning sunlight touches the valley floor. SCOTT T. SMITH

Winter magnifies the differences in texture and tone between rock and water along the Merced River. SCOTT T. SMITH

Drifts of morning fog follow the flow of the Merced River through Yosemite Valley. DENNIS FLAHERTY

" On frosty winter mornings, traces of ice frame Yosemite's waterfalls in white lace, and streams bob with tiny bergs of delicate frazil ice—frozen spray blown off the falls and beaten into frothy mounds. Worry lines of snow crease the faces of granite walls. In winter, Yosemite National Park becomes not only more tranquil but also more ethereal. "

Lora J. Finnegan

A mule deer is momentarily camouflaged against a granite boulder. KENNAN WARD

Snow and fog wrap Sentinel Rock in a solemn and profound silence.   WILLIAM NEILL / LARRY ULRICH STOCK

For a great tree death comes as a gradual transformation. Its vitality ebbs slowly. Even when life has abandoned it entirely it remains a majestic thing. On some hilltop a dead tree may dominate the landscape for miles around. Alone among living things it retains its character and dignity after death.

Edwin Way Teale

65

Even in death, this Jeffrey pine atop Sentinel Dome cuts a classic figure. WILLIAM NEILL / LARRY ULRICH STOCK

The intimacy of rock and water is caught by the reflection of Fletcher Peak in Vogelsang Lake. LONDIE G. PADELSKY

Pausing along the Vogelsang Pass Trail, a horseman enjoys a view of Gallison Lake. LONDIE G. PADELSKY

The beauty of the Merced River resounds in Echo Valley. LONDIE G. PADELSKY

Since 1899, Curry Village has welcomed visitors to Yosemite with a blend of down-home hospitality and family fun. LONDIE G. PADELSKY

One could live with Yosemite, camp in it, tramp in it, winter and summer in it, and find nature in her tender and human, almost domestic moods, as well as in her grand and austere.

John Burroughs

From the Merced River, paddlers enjoy a unique view of Cathedral Rocks.   THOMAS E. GAMACHE

The signature of Yosemite is written in its breathtaking waterfalls.   RON SANFORD

Lightning dances to thunderous applause over Tenaya Creek. KENNAN WARD

The contented burble of Happy Isles is a contrast to the turbulence
of Vernal Fall upstream. NICK FEDRICK

Harbingers of spring, the flowers of dogwoods erupt even before the leaves develop.   LAURENCE PARENT

A showily attired Pacific dogwood dances attendance on the Merced River. JULIEN HAVAC / GNASS PHOTO IMAGES

Dogwood blossoms flicker like candle flames in the morning breeze. JEFF FOOTT

Hikers enjoy a serene moment in the popular backcountry around Cathedral Peak.   LONDIE G. PADELSKY

" I have always traveled the mountain trail on foot, and, traveling so, every rise, every down grade, every stretch of dusty sunshine, every cool shadow becomes important and noteworthy. "

Albert W. Palmer

A male mountain bluebird shares the color of a perfect day.   SHERM SPOELSTRA

Hikers are cradled among the massive buttresses of this giant sequoia, one of the oldest and largest tree species in the world.   JEFF FOOTT

Kolana Rock towers over the calm waters of Hetch Hetchy Reservoir, which stretches behind O'Shaughnessy Dam.   LARRY CARVER

Hetch Hetchy Reservoir helps to satisfy San Francisco's thirst for water. THOMAS E. GAMACHE

At Waterwheel Falls on the Tuolumne River, pinwheels of spray form when the river strikes rocky obstructions. JEFF FOOTT

" By such a river it is impossible to believe that one will ever be tired or old. Every sense applauds it. Taste it, feel its chill on the teeth: it is purity absolute. Watch its racing current, its steady renewal of force: it is transient and eternal. "

Wallace Stegner

A recipe for fun: Take glacially polished granite, add
water, tilt, and slide!   PETER NOEBELS

Defying gravity, a climber leads a roof pitch in Tuolumne Meadows.   BILL HATCHER

" One should sleep on the brink of that Valley, dream of it all night, and drop down into it on the wings of morning. "

Charles Warren Stoddard

A climber tries to nap on a portable ledge while soloing on El Capitan.   BILL HATCHER

Climbers are dwarfed by "The Nose," an imposing route on El Capitan's southwest face.   BILL HATCHER

The Tioga Meadows area is known for its kettles—small lakes or ponds that fill depressions created by glacial melt. LARRY CARVER

Backpackers hike single file along the Grand Canyon of the Tuolumne River. KENNAN WARD

Enthusiastic young hikers step out along the John Muir Trail on their way to high-country adventure.   LONDIE G. PADELSKY

A bird's-eye-view of the Yosemite Lodge area reveals the sinuous curves of the Merced River and the valley road. JEFF FOOTT

    We come here to gain the richness, quietness, and content of the earth, through paths of leaf-mould and bark-mould, in half-swampy stretches through the shady wood. There is always the living richness of contrast. Each elevation has its own growths and personality. But continually, all around, are symbols of grim stateliness and character, because the free processes of unhampered nature flow here, producing this unimpeded loveliness.

Cedric Wright

Spartan quarters house a Yosemite employee, but, oh, what a great backyard to play in! LONDIE G. PADELSKY

Built in the late 1800s, the stately Wawona Hotel continues to provide luxurious accommodations today. LAURENCE PARENT

Yosemite visitors can "rough it" by staying in one of these historic cottages at the Wawona Hotel. THOMAS E. GAMACHE

From the Wawona Hotel, a short stroll over the river and through the bridge leads to the Pioneer Yosemite History Center.   LONDIE G. PADELSKY

      " *Long ago observers of the American scene noted that national parks are for Americans what castles and cathedrals are for Europeans. They are America's national shrines, where its natural treasures of mountains, rivers, and trees are kept and protected. It is understandable, then, why Galen Clark, early park commissioner and Guardian, called Yosemite the* sanctum sanctorum *of the Sierra Nevada—the holy of holies.* "

David Robertson

A firefighter keeps an eye on the progress of a prescribed burn set by the National Park Service to assure the ecological health of the forest.   LONDIE G. PADELSKY

Fire is an integral component of Yosemite's ecosystem.
DENNIS FLAHERTY

Scarred trees stand in mute testimony to the raging power of a wildfire. JEAN CARTER / GNASS PHOTO IMAGES

" *In the forest there is sometimes, you think, a buzzing, almost a rasping among the trees. It is a soothing and yet intriguing sound that comes from nowhere and everywhere. Sometimes it is the distorted echo of running water. Sometimes it is the wind in the treetops. And sometimes it is nothing you can name.* "

Colin Fletcher

" There are falls of water elsewhere finer, there are more stupendous rocks, more beetling cliffs, there are deeper and more awful chasms.... It is in no scene or scenes the charm consists, but in the miles of scenery where cliffs of awful height and rocks of vast magnitude and of varied and exquisite coloring, are banked and fringed and draped and shadowed by the tender foliage of noble and lovely trees and bushes, reflected from the most placid pools, and associated with the most tranquil meadows, the most playful streams, and every variety of soft and peaceful pastoral beauty. "

Frederick Law Olmsted

90

A golden-mantled ground squirrel pauses to scan for predators.   SHERM SPOELSTRA

In the Grand Canyon of the Tuolomne, a transitory pool reflects a nearby cliff. KATHLEEN NORRIS COOK

Lemmon's paintbrushes add color to a pastoral scene in Tuolomne Meadows below Lembert Dome.   LARRY ULRICH

" So extravagant is Nature with her choicest treasures, spending plant beauty as she spends sunshine, pouring it forth into land and sea, garden and desert. "

John Muir

Hummingbirds pollinate paintbrushes, while bees prefer lupines. LONDIE G. PADELSKY

The saprophytic snow plant erupts from the forest floor soon after the snow melts. LONDIE G. PADELSKY

Graceful California poppies unfurl translucent petals.
KENNAN WARD

These earth-bound shooting stars will not flame out in the alpine air. LONDIE G. PADELSKY

Lopsided Lembert Dome, created by glaciers, wears a dark robe of conifers as it presides over a stretch of the Tuolumne River. WILLIAM NEILL / LARRY ULRICH STOCK

❝ What an impression of mass and of power and of grandeur in repose filters into you as you walk along! El Capitan stands there showing its simple sweeping lines through the trees as you approach, like one of the veritable pillars of the firmament.... It is so colossal that it seems near while it is yet far off.... It demands of you a new standard of size which you cannot at once produce.❞

John Burroughs

In the spotlight of the setting sun, El Capitan seems made of gold not granite. KATHLEEN NORRIS COOK

Spindly fireweeds jostle for position over the broader leaves of a thimbleberry. LARRY ULRICH

A mosaic of deciduous alder and maple leaves commemorates the changing of the seasons.
JEAN CARTER / GNASS PHOTO IMAGES

Wood ducks are at home on the water or in trees. SHERM SPOELSTRA

Winter reverently wraps the Gothic forms of Higher and Lower Cathedral Spires in silence. JEFF FOOTT

"Frazil," the frozen spray of cascading water, clings to the wall behind Upper Yosemite Fall.   INGER HOGSTROM

Lower Yosemite Fall dons an ethereal veil of fog on a wintry morning.   NICK FEDRICK

A pair of massive sequoias dwarfs a visitor to the Mariposa Grove Museum.   LAURENCE PARENT

When not closed by snow, Tioga Pass offers the only vehicle access to the park from the east. JON GNASS / GNASS PHOTO IMAGES

A snowman's smile speaks to the child in all of us. JEFF FOOTT

Spring snowmelt from Mammoth Peak washes away the snow banks in Dana Meadows. MARK & JENNIFER MILLER

The Merced River plunges more than 300 feet over Vernal Fall on its way to the valley floor.   JEFF GNASS

Emeric Lake and the Cathedral Range share a reflective moment. LONDIE G. PADELSKY

From atop Bloody Canyon, one can see saltwater Mono Lake shimmering in the distance.   DENNIS FLAHERTY

“ *The Sierra [Range] has dominated my mind, art and spirit. It is quite impossible to explain in words this almost symbiotic relationship.... The juxtaposition of rock, glacial lakes, meadows, forests and streams is extraordinary.* ”

Ansel Adams

The remnant of a whitebark pine strikes a classic pose below Ansel Adams Peak. JOHN DITTLI

Budd Creek gently carves a course through Tuolumne Meadows. JON GNASS / GNASS PHOTO IMAGES

" In the high mountain spring of May or early June, these wet meadows have resounded over the centuries with the mellow trills of Yosemite toads and the krek-it *of tiny Pacific tree frogs."*

Verna R. Johnston

The wonders of Yosemite need not all be grand and imposing. KENNAN WARD

Nature's garden features a riot of Sierra primroses and wall-hugging yellow monkeyflowers.   JOHN DITTLI

they made it possible

Yosemite on My Mind would have been impossible to produce without the keen eyes and technical skills of more than two dozen professional photographers. These women and men submitted their finest images, and the results show in this stunning collection of photos. What does not show is the work it took to get these images—the early mornings to capture the sunrise, the long hikes up mountain trails and through deep snow, the endless hours of waiting for the perfect light, the hundreds of shots that didn't turn out quite right, and the level of technical skill that was acquired through years of experience and study. To all the photographers who contributed to *Yosemite on My Mind*, we says thanks. We appreciate their art and their hard work.

The Publisher

Photographers in *Yosemite on My Mind*

Ken Archer
Larry Carver
Kathleen Norris Cook
John Dittli
Nick Fedrick
Dennis Flaherty
Jeff Foott
John R. Ford
Thomas E. Gamache
Jeff Gnass
Bill Hatcher
Inger Hogstrom
Lee Kline
Mark & Jennifer Miller
Peter Noebels
Londie G. Padelsky
Laurence Parent
Ron Sanford
Richard Hamilton Smith
Scott T. Smith
Sherm Spoelstra
Claude Steelman
Larry Ulrich
Kennan Ward

Gnass Photo Images
    Jean Carter
    Jon Gnass
    Julien Havac
    Christian Heeb
Larry Ulrich Stock
    William Neill

© 2000 by Falcon® Publishing, Inc.
Helena, Montana

All rights reserved, including the right to reproduce any part of this book in any form, except brief quotations for reviews, without the written permission of the publisher.

Design, typesetting, and other prepress work by Falcon Publishing, Inc., Helena, Montana. Printed in Korea.

Library of Congress Number: 00-130166

ISBN 1-56044-970-5

For extra copies of this book please check with your local bookstore, or write Falcon®, P.O. Box 1718, Helena, MT 59624, or call toll-free 1-800-582-2665.
Visit our web site at www.FalconBooks.com.

Front cover photos:
  El Capitan at sunset KATHLEEN NORRIS COOK
  Black bear JOHN R. FORD
Back cover photos:
  Half Dome, Yosemite Valley
    CHRISTIAN HEEB / GNASS PHOTO IMAGES
  Upper Mariposa Grove LARRY ULRICH
  Vernal Fall LONDIE G. PADELSKY
  Climbing Sentinel Rock PETER NOEBELS
End papers: CHRISTIAN HEEB / GNASS PHOTO IMAGES
Design and layout: LAURIE GIGETTE GOULD
Edited by: GAYLE SHIRLEY
Text research: DAMIAN FAGAN

acknowledgments

Title page and pages 56, 87, and 112 quotes from *Yosemite National Park: Nature's Masterpiece in Stone*, by David Robertson. Del Mar, CA: Woodlands Press in conjunction with Yosemite Natural History Association, 1985.

Pages 3 and 13 quotes from *Yosemite Trails: Exploring the High Sierra*, by J. Smeaton Chase. Boston: Houghton Mifflin, 1911.

Page 7 quote from *Land Above the Trees*, by Ann H. Zwinger and Beatrice E. Willard. New York: Harper & Row, 1972.

Pages 8, 20, 36, 48, 55, and 92 quotes from *My First Summer in the Sierra*, by John Muir. Boston: Houghton Mifflin, 1911.

Pages 14 and 31 quotes from *The High Sierra*, by Ezra Bowen and the Editors of Time-Life Books. New York: Time-Life Books, 1972.

Pages 16 and 26 quotes from *Roughing It*, by Mark Twain. New York: Harper & Brothers, 1959. Originally published in 1871.

Page 22 quote from *John Muir: Nature Writings*, by John Muir. New York: Literary Classics of the United States, 1997.

Page 25 quote from *The Great Bear Almanac*, by Gary Brown. New York: Lyons & Burford, 1993.

Pages 29 and 53 quotes from *Our National Parks*, by John Muir. San Francisco: Sierra Club, 1991. Originally published in 1901.

Page 34 quote from "Ski-Experience," by Ansel Adams, in *Voices for the Earth: A Treasury of the Sierra Club Bulletin*, 1893-1977, ed. by Ann Gilliam. San Francisco: Sierra Club Books, 1979.

Page 44 quote from *Yosemite Official National Park Handbook*, produced by the National Park Service. Washington, DC: U.S. Department of the Interior, 1990.

Page 58 quote from "Serenity in Yosemite," by Lewis P. Mansfield, in *Voices for the Earth: A Treasury of the Sierra Club Bulletin*, 1893-1977, ed. by Ann Gilliam. San Francisco: Sierra Club Books, 1979.

Page 62 quote from "The Other Yosemite," by Lora J. Finnegan. *Sunset*, November 1997.

Page 64 quote from *Dune Boy: The Early Years of a Naturalist*, by Edwin Way Teale. New York: Dodd, Mead & Company, 1943.

Pages 68, 80, and 94 quotes from *Yosemite: Its Discovery, Its Wonders, and Its People*, by Margaret Sanborn. New York: Random House, 1981.

Page 74 quote from *The Mountain Trail and Its Message*, by Albert W. Palmer. Boston: The Pilgrim Press, 1911.

Page 78 quote from *The Sound of Mountain Water*, by Wallace Stegner. New York: Doubleday, 1969. Originally published in 1946.

Page 83 quote from *Yosemite: Valley of Thunder*, by Ann Zwinger. San Francisco: HarperCollins, 1996.

Page 84 quote from "Trail Song: Giant Forest and Vicinity," by Cedric Wright, in *Voices for the Earth: A Treasury of the Sierra Club Bulletin*, 1893-1977, ed. by Ann Gilliam. San Francisco: Sierra Club Books, 1979.

Page 89 quote from *The Thousand-Mile Summer*, by Colin Fletcher. Berkeley: Howell-North Books, 1964.

Page 90 quote from "Yosemite and the Mariposa Grove: A Preliminary Report, 1865," by Frederick Law Olmsted. *Landscape Architecture*, October 1952.

Page 106 quote from *Yosemite and the Range of Light*, by Ansel Adams. Boston: New York Graphics Society, 1979.

Page 108 quote from *Sierra Nevada: The Naturalist's Companion*, by Verna R. Johnston. Berkeley: University of California Press, 1998.

Half Dome and Tenaya Canyon bid another glorious Sierra day adieu. WILLIAM NEILL / LARRY ULRICH STOCK

" While Yosemite's immediate appeal is to the senses, its final appeal is to the spirit. "

David Robertson